САНДАРДЫҢ ХИКАЯСЫ

THE NUMBER STORY

SMALL BOOK ONE

ENGLISH - KAZAKH

*Numbers Teach Children
Their Number Names*

written and illustrated by

MISS ANNA

Early Reader Edition of *The Number Story 1*
Bronze Medal Winner, 2016 Wishing Shelf Book Award

Library of Congress Control Number: 2018902040

Names: Miss Anna, author.
Title: Number story : numbers teach children their number names / Miss Anna.
Description: Portland, OR: Lumpy Publishing, 2018.
Identifiers: ISBN 978-1-945977-70-1| LCCN 2018902040
Summary: The pictures and rhymes present stories which introduce numbers 0-10.
Subjects: LCSH Numeration—English--Kazakh--Pictorial works--Juvenile literature. | BISAC JUVENILE NONFICTION /
Languages: English--Kazakh
Classification: LCC QA141.3 .M57 2018 | DDC 513—dc23

Publisher: Lumpy Publishing
Website: www.missannabooks.com
Email: missanna@missannabooks.com

Paperback: ISBN 978-1-945977-70-1
Printed in the U.S.A.   1 3 5 7 9 10 8 6 4 2

Сандардың атауларын оқып білгіңіз келе ме?

It is very easy and a lot of fun!

Бұл өте оңай және көңілді!

Say-along our little jingle

Бізбен бірге әндет!

starting from Number One!

Біз Бір Санынан бастаймыз!

1

ONE looks like my one finger.

БІР

Менің бір саусағым сияқты.

ONE!
БІР!

2

TWO trails a tail.

ЕКІ

Оның артынан ерген
құйрығы бар.

A TAIL! ҚҰЙРЫҚ!

3

THREE has bumps.

ҮШ

Оның дөңбешіктері бар.

Мына жасыл
дөнбешіктерге қара!

4

FOUR carries a sail.

ТӨРТ

Қайық сияқты желкені бар.

A SAIL!
ЖЕЛКЕН!
Желкені бар қайық!

5

FIVE   is a racing track.

БЕС

Бұл жарысқа арналған жол.

VROOM
ВРУУУМ!
1

6

SIX curves like a snail.

АЛТЫ

Бұл ұлу сияқты оралымдар.

A SNAIL! УЛУ!

7

SEVEN has a sharp angle.

ЖЕТІ
Бұның өткір бұрышы бар.

BE CAREFUL! IT'S SHARP!

Абай бол! Бұл өте өткір ғой!

8

EIGHT is rollercoaster rails.

СЕГІЗ

Бұл жарысқа арналған жолақтар.

АЛАҚАЙ!
YIPPEE!

NINE   is a bubble on a stick.

ТОҒЫЗ

Бұл таяқшадағы көпіршік қой.

A BUBBLE! КӨПІРШІК!

10

TEN is an eye of a whale.

ОН

Бұл киттің көзі.

HELLO!
СӘЛЕМ!

And
Және

0

ZERO   is an empty pail.

НӨЛ
Бұл бос шелек.

IT'S
EMPTY!
Бұл Бос!

Thank you for playing with us today.

We had a lot of fun too!

Бізбен бүгін ойнағаныңыз үшін рахмет.

Біз де өте көңілді уақыт өткіздік!

We are your Number friends,
Zero to Ten,
Who will be here for you~

Біз сіздің сандық достарыңызбыз

Нөлден Онға дейін.

Біз мұнда әрдайым

сіз үшін боламыз ~

Bye-bye now!
See you again soon!

Қазірге сау бол!

Келесі кездескенше!

The Numbers are *SINGING* too!

To sing-a-long, look for Miss Anna Number Story
at your favorite music store like iTUNES.

MP3

Numbers 0-10
IDENTIFYING & COUNTING

Numbers 11-20
& Ordinals
first, second, third...

Numbers 0-100
& Place Values
ones, tens, hundreds...

About Clocks
& Telling Time
hours, minutes, seconds

Number Story 1 & 2
isbn: 978-0-996216-48-7

Number Story 3 & 4
isbn: 978-1-945977-01-5

Number Story 5 & 6
isbn: 978-1-945977-06-0

Number Story 7 & 8
isbn: 978-1-949320-40-4

For more Miss Anna books to love,
visit us at

www.missannabooks.com

Numbers are working hard all over the world!
Come Travel the World with Us!